BASIS FOR MOTIVATION AND CHANGE

By: Robert DuPrey Ph.D.

- ‣ Concepts Behind Motivation
- ‣ Organizational Change
- ‣ Social Aspect of Change
- ‣ Denial and Acceptance

By: Robert DuPrey, Ph.D.

BASIS FOR MOTIVATION AND CHANGE

Order this book online at www.trafford.com
or email orders@trafford.com

Most Trafford titles are also available at major online book retailers.

Book design by Robert DuPrey
Cover design and illustration by Robert DuPrey

Printed in Victoria, BC, Canada.

ISBN: 978-1-4269-2300-5 (Soft)

*Our mission is to efficiently provide the world's finest, most comprehensive
book publishing service, enabling every author to experience success.
To find out how to publish your book, your way, and have it available
worldwide, visit us online at www.trafford.com*

Trafford rev. 11/17/2009

 www.trafford.com

North America & international
toll-free: 1 888 232 4444 (USA & Canada)
phone: 250 383 6864 ♦ fax: 812 355 4082

I dedicate this book to my father.

Basis of Motivation

Introduction

Motivation as a form of human resources development can be tailored into a greater and more positive work environment. With the United States economy becoming ever more interdependent on the global economy, motivation of professionals and an understanding of employee behavior in the workplace have taken on even greater importance. Among various behavioral theories embraced by American businesses are those of Frederick Herzberg, Clayton Alderfer and Abraham Maslow. Herzberg, a psychologist, proposed a theory about job factors that motivate employees. Maslow, a behavioral scientist, developed a theory about the rank and satisfaction of various human needs. Alderfer is known for his "Existence, Relatedness and Growth" theory, also known as

ERG theory.

This section first reviews and introduces the motivation theories of Alderfer, Maslow, and Herzberg separately. Second, this section will compare and contrast theories and will discuss advantages and disadvantages of each theory. Finally, the writer will conclude with a summary.

Motivation Theories

Motivation is one of the constructs psychologists have propounded in their quest for understanding the individual. The word is derived from the Latin verb movere, which means, "to move" (Webster's New World Dictionary of America, 1988, p. 889). The inner drive, the urge or the desire of the person to do something, is also called motivation.

Maslow Needs Hierarchy

Maslow's hierarchy of needs model provides a hierarchical framework for organizing human needs. Schwartz (1983) writes, "Maslow's hierarchy is reinterpreted in a way that is consistent with Maslow's own characterizations of his hierarchy as psychodynamic, psychoanalytic, and a hierarchy of character types" (pp. 203-214).

Maslow (1980) defines the motivation theory as "Motivation = summation valence x expectancy" (p. 21) where, summation is "the process of adding or totaling" (American Heritage Dictionary, 1985, p. 1218), valence is "a person's preference for a particular outcome" (American Heritage Dictionary, 1985, p. 1335), and expectancy is "an expected amount calculated on the basis of statistical probability" (American Heritage Dictionary, 1985, p. 476).

Maslow centered his theory of motivation on what he called the hierarchy of human needs. "Hierarchy of needs is the inborn array of physiological and psychological needs encompassing the basic needs and metaneeds. As a lower need is fulfilled with us, a new and higher need tends to emerge" (Maslow, 1943, p. 396). In essence, he contended, "every person is born with a set of basic needs encompassing physiological needs for safety, belongingness or love, and self-esteem" (Maslow, 1967, p. 279). In a complex but lucid formulation he argued that these basic needs could be seen as making up "an unfolding hierarchy" (Maslow, 1942, p. 331).

Maslow identified five basic needs or motives that he believes are common in all mentally healthy adults.

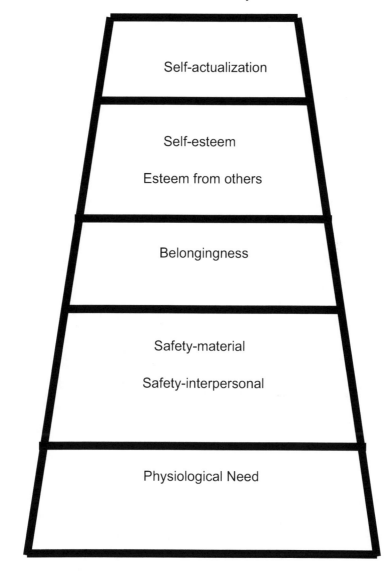

Maslow
Needs Hierarchy

Self-actualization

Self-esteem

Esteem from others

Belongingness

Safety-material

Safety-interpersonal

Physiological Need

The first level of the hierarchy needs is "physiological needs" (Maslow, 1943, p. 370). Physiological needs relate to hunger, thirst and sex. Maslow (1943) writes: In the human being who is missing everything in life in an extreme fashion, it is most likely that the major motivation would be the physiological needs rather than any others. A person who is lacking food, safety, love, and esteem would most probably hunger for food more strongly than for anything else ... all other needs may become simply non-existent or be pushed into the background. (p. 373)

The second level of his hierarchy is the "safety needs," for protection against danger, threat, or deprivation. Maslow (1943) broadened the view of stability and safety by including the human preference for familiar things, as opposed to the unfamiliar. "The tendency to have some religion that organizes the universe and the men in it into some sort of satisfactory, coherent, meaningful whole is also in part motivated by safety-seeking" (Maslow, 1943, p. 379).

The third level in the hierarchy is "belongingness and love needs" (Maslow, 1943, p. 50). Love needs are for satisfactory association with others, for belonging to groups, and for giving and receiving friendship and affection. Maslow (1954) writes, Sex may be studied as a purely physiological need. Ordinarily sexual behavior is multi-determined, that is to say determined not only by sexual but also by other needs, chief among which are the love and affection needs. Also not to be overlooked is the fact that the love needs involve both giving and receiving love (p. 90).

The fourth level is the "self-esteem" (Maslow, 1943, p. 372). Esteem needs for self-respect and for the respect of others is often referred to as ego or status needs. Maslow (1943) classified these needs into two basic categories: the first category is defined as "the desire for strength, for achievement, for adequacy, for confidence in the face of the world, and for independence and freedom" (p. 381), and the second category is defined as "the desire for reputation or prestige, recognition, attention, importance, or appreciation" (p. 382).

The highest level in the hierarchy of needs is "self-actualization needs" (Maslow, 1943, p. 373). Self-actualization or self-fulfillment needs were created to achieve the potential within a person for maximum self-development, and for creativity and self-expression. Maslow (1954) points out that all people in society have a "need or desire for stable, firmly based, usually high evaluation of themselves, for self-respect, or self-esteem, and for esteem of others" (p. 90). Maslow speculated that higher needs might become the prime motivation for a self-actualized individual, superseding the more common egocentric desires for self-esteem, possessions (Maslow, 1968). Maslow explains that by combining the employee's needs with those of the organization, the savvy manager can create an equitable psychological contract formed to satisfy both sides in the organization (Maslow, 1973).

Maslow contends that these needs arranged themselves in a distinct order of importance and that the appearance of one's needs usually rested on the prior satisfaction of other more pre-potent needs. He explains "self-actualization" as, The apex of personal growth, in which we become freed from basic needs and deficiency-motivation, not an end point in most people, but a drive or yearning to fully develop. Also the process of fulfilling our latent talents, capacities, and potentialities at any time, in any amount. Although we all have drive, we also posses a fear of growth. (Maslow, 1957, pp. 17-22).

Alderfer ERG Theory

Alderfer summarizes human needs in terms of three basic categories. There are "existence, relatedness, and growth" (Alderfer, 1969, p. 142)). Since the Existence, Relatedness and Growth (ERG) theory was developed based on Maslow's hierarchical needs theory, it has some similarities with Maslow's theory. In the ERG theory, there are three core needs, instead of Maslow's five core needs, that a person strives to meet: "the existence needs; the relatedness needs and the growth needs" (Alderfer, 1969, p. 142). According to Alderfer (1969) "existence needs include material and physiological needs and desires that can be satisfied by air, water, money and working conditions" (pp. 174-175). The "relatedness needs," he explains, "include needs of relationships with significant others". This need is substantially different from the other needs, because "the process of satisfaction for existence needs prohibits mutual relationships" (Alderfer, 1969, p. 147).

Satisfaction of the needs depends on a process of sharing or mutuality, whose elements are exchange of acceptance, confirmation, understanding, and influence. The "relatedness needs" include exchange or expression of anger and hostility as well as positive needs such as friendship. The "growth needs" include all needs involving creative efforts. The growth needs are crucial in Alderfer's view, since they create "a greater sense of wholeness and fullness as a human being by satisfying growth needs" (Alderfer, 1969, p. 147). Schwartz (1983) writes, "Alderfer's theory requires further research and testing to evaluate the three level motivation theory" (p.203). According to Alderfer (1975) "the prepotency or rank of ERG categories is neither universal nor predictable; it differs from person to person as a function of culture, education, family background, age ... neither the sequence nor the salience of these needs can, therefore, be generalized to all individuals" (pp. 510-511).

Alderfer
ERG

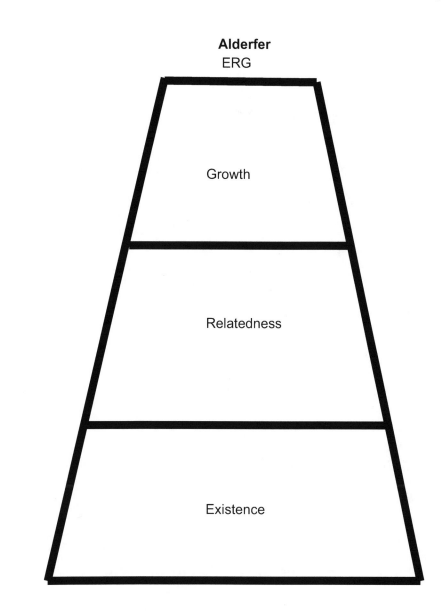

Herzberg Two-Factor Theory

Herzberg's two-factor theory of motivation, also known as motivator-hygiene theory (Herzberg, 1959), added an additional dimension to motivation theory and focused attention on motivation in the workplace. Herzberg explains that the hygiene factors acted in a manner that was "analogous to medical hygiene" (Herzberg, Monsner & Snyderman, 1959, p.113). The hygiene worked "to remove the health hazards from the environment of man" (Herzberg, et al., 1959, p.113). Herzberg views hygiene as taking on a preventative rather than curative role (Herzberg, 1966). Since individuals are much more sensitive to a lack of satisfaction of the lower order needs than they are to the satisfaction of these needs, organizations have focused much of their attention to satisfying lower order needs with the expected outcome of increased performance.

Herzberg's two-factor theory supports Maslow's hierarchy of self-actualization by adding an additional dimension to his theory that is focused on motivation in the workplace in the form of satisfier. Herzberg defines that satisfiers or motivators can create growth and job enrichment. He also determines that the motivators were elements that enriched a person's job. Morgan (2000) writes, "Herzberg's two-factor theory was based on the work of Maslow and developed from research on accountants and engineers to determine the satisfying and dissatisfying factors about their work" (p. 32). Morgan (2000) concluded, "There was a strong support for Herzberg's hypothesis that factors accounted for job motivation was different from the factors accounted for job dissatisfaction" (p. 32). Herzberg posited that the factors that resulted in work satisfaction included "achievements, recognition, work itself, responsibility, advancement and growth" (Herzberg, 1959, p. 111). Herzberg identified the following factors as resulting in worker dissatisfaction: "salary, possibility of growth, interpersonal relations with subordinates, status, interpersonal relations with superiors, interpersonal relations with peers, supervision, company policy, working conditions, personal life and job security" (Herzberg, 1959, p. 7).

Herzberg
Motivator-Hygiene

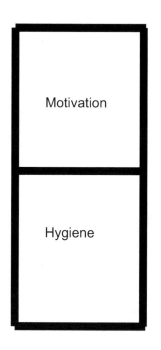

Herzberg's studies revealed that the strongest satisfying

factors or "motivators" had to do directly with the person's

particular job "results, achievements, recognition, work itself,

work as an interesting activity, responsibility, and

advancement" (Herzberg, 1959, p. 111). Potentially negative

factors in motivation are: "company policy and administration, supervision, pay, interpersonal relations and working conditions" (Herzberg, 1959, p. 111). Company policy and administration, which Herzberg called "the single most important factor in determining bad feelings about a job" (Herzberg, 1959, p. 7) are part of initial organizational settings.

Herzberg (1959) suggests that "motivation is a result of personal growth and is based on an innate and compelling need to grow" (p. 7). This means that people find satisfaction in performing tasks that are interesting and challenging. These feelings allow individuals to realize their potentiality or to become the best that they can be. The desire to fulfill personal potential propels the individual to see growth and provides the incentive to achieve. Herzberg (1959) writes: Given an individual operating from a neutral point, with neither positive nor negative attitudes towards his job, the satisfaction of the factors, which we may call the satisfiers

would increase his job satisfaction beyond the neutral point.

The absence of satisfaction to these factors would merely

drop him back to this neutral level but would not turn him into

a dissatisfied employee. (p. 111)

Herzberg (1976) believes that individual interests should

be adapted to increase motivation, morale, and productivity,

thereby reducing employee turnover and alienation within the

organization. As a result of changing motivational values and

areas of authority within an organization setting, there is a

growing interest to apply many human resource practices in

an effort to increase accountability. Lacey (2000) writes,

"Herzberg claimed that his theory could provide insight into

what motivates employees to excel in their jobs while other

seemingly better off employees lack the motivation to perform

to their potential" (p. 5).

Compare and Contrast theories

Maslow's hierarchy is a good model because it not only provides a relatively simple framework for organizing needs, but it can also help people consider the relative importance of different needs level as they plan strategies and points of intervention (Lacey, 2000). Herzberg's theory, in other hand, is based on two separate and distinct sets of needs; motivators and hygienes. Maslow writes, People who have enough basic [need] satisfaction to look for love and respect (rather than just food and safety) tend to develop such qualities as loyalty, friendliness, and civic consciousness, and to become better parents, teachers, [and] public servants ... People living at the level of self-actualization are, in fact, found simultaneously to love mankind most and to be the most developed idiosyncratically (Maslow, 1958, pp. 51-56).

Maslow's theory may apply to individuals under normal

circumstances. But it is questionable if it can be applied to most people who are business owners or the fired executive who goes without basic needs (safety and food) but still belongs to his country club. In contrast to Maslow's theory, Herzberg's theory can be applied to individuals such as engineers, accountings and managers. The most significant contribution of the motivator-hygiene theory of Herzberg has been its impact on business and other organizations in the form of job enrichment programs. In comparing Herzberg to Maslow one can find that Maslow defines self-esteem as "the desire for strength, for achievement, for adequacy, for mastery and competence, for confidence in the face of the world, and for independence and freedom" (Maslow, 1970, p. 45). Herzberg, on the other hand, defines "motivators" as sets of achievement, responsibility, advancement and personal growth. In Maslow's view, one needs to systematically pass four stages of needs in the hierarchy in order to reach the self-esteem level. In contrast to Maslow five level of needs hierarchy, Herzberg defines only one level of satisfaction and motivation that is intrinsic to the work itself. Herzberg first identifies the need for achievement, which reflects "an individual's desire to do something more effectively than in the past ... the need for power is the desire to be influential in a group and to control one's environment" (Herzberg, 1959, p. 111).

The absence of hygiene factors can create job dissatisfaction, but their presence does not motivate or create satisfaction (Herzberg, 1966). There are similarities in Herzberg and Alderfer theories. Alderfer determines the absence of existence needs can create job dissatisfaction such as working conditions and money. Herzberg concluded that hygiene factors such as pay and working conditions could prevent dissatisfaction but do not contribute to an employee's motivation. Instead, Herzberg concluded that the nature of the work itself was related to motivation on the job.

According a research by Davisson (1997) he revealed, "If hygiene factors are added to a job setting, dissatisfaction will be reduced ... the motivators are related to high satisfaction and willingness to work harder ... when present, these motivation factors induce people to work harder, but their absence does not produce job dissatisfaction" (p. 18). In Davission's view motivators were associated with long-term positive effects in job performance, while the hygiene factors consistently produced only short-term changes in job attitudes and performance, which quickly fell back to their previous levels.

Alderfer growth needs also supports Maslow's self-actualization. In contrast to Maslow and Herzberg, Alderfer attempted to reformulate the need hierarchy in three stages and individuals can reach the self-actualization level (the highest level of self-esteem) by passing two previous stages of needs. Herzberg (1976) writes, Since separate factors needed to be considered, depending on whether job satisfaction or job dissatisfaction is being examined, it follows that these two feelings are not opposites of each other. The opposite of job satisfaction is not job dissatisfaction but, rather, no job satisfaction, and similarly, the opposite of job dissatisfaction is not job satisfaction, but no job dissatisfaction (p. 58).

Alderfer (1972) believes that a person's set of needs is more of a continuum than of hierarchical levels as oppose to Maslow's theory. According to Maslow (1943), "If one's population is faced with lower level needs, strategies to address higher level needs will probably not be very effective" (p. 370). Maslow hypothesizes that lower level needs must be addressed before individuals can move into the next level. In contrast to Maslow's theory, Herzberg defines that individuals can move into motivator or satisfier without going through stages. Maslow (1943) writes, "Human beings are motivated by unsatisfied needs, and that certain lower needs need to be satisfied before higher needs can be satisfied" (p. 50). Whenever a lower level need is not being met, one regresses down the hierarchy to satisfy that unmet need. Lower level needs usually require a more immediate response, thus having higher urgency. "The first premise was that man is a wanting animal and rarely reaches a state of complete satisfaction except for a short time" (Maslow, 1962, p. 69).

While Maslow's theory of needs was not developed specifically for work organizations, Alderfer's theory attempted to establish a conceptualization of human needs that was relevant to organizational settings. Alderfer developed the ERG theory of motivation in response to criticisms of Maslow's hierarchy. Fujii (1999) writes, "Alderfer's three need categories are more clearly defined than Maslow's five categories" (p. 34). The ERG theory has two important differences from Maslow's. The ERG theory suggests that more than one level of needs can cause motivation at the same time. White and Bednar (1986) write, "Alderfer's position reflects a classic frustration-regression reaction ... this is a person frustrated by not being able to achieve a desired goal may find satisfaction by displacing the goal and turning personal energy to something already achieved" (p. 246). The ERG theory of Alderfer suggests that if "needs remain unsatisfied at some high level, the individual will become frustrated, regress to a lower level, and begin to pursue lower level needs again" (Alderfer, 1974, p. 507).

Alderfer's ERG theory does not assume a rigid hierarchy such as Maslow's. His ERG theory accounts for differences in need preferences between cultures better than Maslow's need hierarchy. Another feature of Alderfer's ERG theory is that when higher needs are frustrated, then lower needs return, even if they were once already satisfied. Alderfer identifies an almost inherent need for achievement.

"If an individual has a high need for achievement, he will solve the problems that may have arisen from redundancy and set out moderately difficult goals to achieve" (Alderfer, 1974, p. 507). He further continues "individuals with the high need for achievement will usually achieve them" (Alderfer, 1974, p. 507). They will put everything they have into making a success of things. However, there is an interesting psychological problem. Such individuals have a need for feedback. They need to be told how well they are doing.

Alderfer (1977) writes, "A corporate commitment to quality that is not based on intrinsic motivation is a house built on sand" (p. 223). Alderfer tested Maslow's theory and challenged Maslow's hypothesis that lower level needs do not necessarily take priority over higher level needs. For example, some persons may refuse basic assistance (food stamps) because accepting such assistance challenges their perception of self and often alters their status among their peers (Maslow, 1959).

Alderfer (1973) points out that some of "Maslow's needs hierarchy theory overlapped with other parts of his theory" (p. 438). He mentions that "the safety needs and physiological needs and belongingness needs of Maslow are overlapping (Alderfer, 1989, p. 439). He further explains, "the safety needs which deal with the physiological aspect into existence needs, and those, which relate to belongingness into relatedness needs" (Alderfer, 1989, p. 351). The same applied to "the esteem needs, which depend on reactions from others, were categorized to the relatedness needs" and those that relate to "self-fulfill ness were categorized into growth needs" (Alderfer, 1989, p. 351).

The theories of Herzberg and Maslow were frequently integrated in many research studies due to their similarities such as Herzberg's motivator (satisfier) and Maslow's self-esteem. This enabled one to get a clear understanding of how and why people are motivated to work. Chen (1997) in his research study reveals, "Motivating needs all seem to be task oriented and they may apply to almost any managerial, leadership or even business situations" (p. 38). Several commonalties were found when the theories of both Maslow and Herzberg were compared. For instance, the motivator needs corresponded closely with the higher order needs of esteem and self-actualization in the Maslow hierarchy. The love and belonging needs were found to be partially related to motivators of Herzberg's theory. The hygienic needs of Herzberg theory, which included the physiological, safety and portion of the love and belonging needs, were regarded as potential dissatisfiers rather than sources of motivation. Gray and Starks (1988) write, "perhaps the most basic similarity between the Maslow hierarchy of needs and the Herzberg two-factor theory is that both assume specific needs energize behavior" (p. 115).

The difference between Maslow's and Alderfer's needs theory is their view of the hierarchy model. Alderfer describes that these needs arranged only in the sense of increasing abstractness (Alderfer, 1972). In other words, moving from the existence needs to the growth needs, the need increases its abstractness and decreases its concreteness. Although Alderfer agrees with Maslow that unsatisfied needs motivate individuals to meet the needs, he claims that one may focus on the lower needs when one gets frustrated in efforts to satisfy higher needs. An example of this is when one who cannot meet the growth needs focuses on satisfying more concrete needs, "the relatedness or the existence needs" (Alderfer, 1969, p. 4). Alderfer calls this process frustration regression and insists that satisfaction progression and frustration regression (Alderfer, 1972) coexist among three needs.

In contrast to Maslow's needs theory, Alderfer's ERG theory claims that each need does not become less important once the need is satisfied. But Maslow explains that the need does become less important once it is met. As for Herzberg's two-factor theory, the dissatisfiers (hygiene factors) and the satisfiers (motivators) are not simply opposites, but rather like sensations in the same way as pain and pleasure. A research study by McCarthy (1997) reveals that Herzberg emphasized, "Satisfaction was not the opposite of dissatisfaction on a continuum" (pp. 21-22). Based on Herzberg's (1982) theory, satisfiers describe a person's relationship with what she or he does, may relate to the tasks being performed. Dissatisfiers, on the other hand, have to do with a person's relationship to the context or environment in which she or he performs the job (Herzberg, 1966).

The failure to find support for Maslow's need categories in an organizational setting is due to an inadequate conceptualization, which does not readily facilitate the development of operational indicators (Schneider, Benjamin, Alderfer and Clayton, 1973). Maslow's theory ignores the significance of individual differences and fails to distinguish the difference between what people "value" and what their "needs" are (White & Bednar, 1986). Needs such as esteem, and self-actualization are important to the content of work motivation although the exact nature of these needs and how they are related to motivation are not clear (Luthans, 1985). Lawler (1973) summarizes " ... in general, people are somewhat more concerned with satisfying higher-order needs than they used to be" (p. 25).

Maslow was also criticized for fear of conducting empirical research. He had indeed pointed the way in motivation and personality to "dozens of intriguing and potentially important avenues of humanistic research" (Schwartz, 1983, p. 203), but he was not personally involved in that kind of empirical work. The truth was that he simply did

not accept the responsibility of serving as guide and mentor

to advanced graduate students, and he decided that

conducting empirical research would draw valuable time and

energy away from his quest to transform psychology's

purview (Schwartz, 1983, p. 214).

The negative side of manipulating the Herzberg's two-

factor theory and the hygiene factors of job performance is

that it is more costly and less effective than manipulating the

motivators. The hygiene climate of the organization is not

nearly as important for innovation as the motivator potential of

actual jobs the people do (Herzberg, 1987). The principal

drawbacks to job enrichment are the expense, training time

and the loss of routine. Herzberg (1987) suggests the job

should be arranged so the worker gets a "kick out of doing it"

(p. 109).

Critics predicted that Herzberg's job enrichment concept would reduce the number of employees (Bowen, 1980). Ironically, the recent restructuring and down sizing of companies has often produced job enrichment. With fewer employees performing the same tasks, some job enrichment is inevitable. Herzberg has found that greater efficiency of enriched jobs ultimately leads to a competitive edge and more jobs (Herzberg, 1987). Other limitations are ignoring and minimizing individual differences and assuming all persons are alike.

Alderfer's theory was also questioned based on the concept of "individual differences" (Alderfer, 1969, p. 170). Individuals have basic needs and they enact their environments and they enact them variously and systematically according to their needs (Alderfer, 1972). Alderfer rejects the idea that human beings can enact environments (Weick, 1969). Alderfer concludes that if both existence and relatedness needs are relatively dissatisfied, then fewer growth needs are satisfied (Alderfer, 1972). This might be true in many cases, but if an individual's basic needs are not satisfied, the growth needs and even some of the relatedness needs cannot be satisfied at all.

Motivation Conclusion

Content theories of Maslow, Herzberg and Alderfer emphasize the importance of inner needs in motivation. They focused on the existence of these needs and their role in initiating the motivational cycle. Unfortunately, most theories share the same assumptions that limit their usefulness to managers and organizations (Schwartz, 1983). All theories assume that all employees are alike, all situations are alike and there is one best way to motivate all employees.

Although Herzberg's paradigm of hygiene and motivating factors and Maslow's hierarchy of needs may still have broad applicability in the business world, at least one aspect of each, "salary as a hygiene factor" (Herzberg, 1959, p. 111) and "esteem as a lower order need than self-actualization" (Herzberg, 1959, p. 111), may not seem to hold in some cases, such as safety in the workplace. These findings may begin to explain why good workers are being lost to other, higher paying positions and to help administrators focus more closely on the esteem needs of employees, individually and collectively. Angielczyk (1997) writes, "employees may consider hygiene factors like pay and good working conditions as a right of employment but are not satisfied or motivated to improve performance by these elements" (p. 7). Oleson (1999) revealed, "When it comes to attitudes toward money, social scientists stray from the economist's assumption that decision making is rational and uniform" (pp. 13-14). He continued, "uniform behavior would require that all consumers share the same attitudes, values, and beliefs toward money and its use" (pp. 13-14). Organizations need to first recognize the factors that lead to both job satisfaction and motivation.

All three theories of motivation have their own strengths and limitations. Maslow's needs hierarchy theory is easy to understand and is intuitively appealing but ignores the significance of individual differences (White & Bednar, 1986). The underlying premise of Alderfer's ERG theory reduces Maslow's hierarchy to three general-need categories and failure to satisfy a need that may lead to overemphasis on lower needs. White et al. (1986) summarize the strength of ERG theory and writes that it "received empirical support" but needs "further research and testing" (p. 259). Regarding Herzberg and his theory, certain factors related to the nature of work are responsible for motivation, and other factors related to the work environment may attract and hold workers but do not motivate them. On the weak side of his theory, it ignores and minimizes individual differences and assumes all persons are alike and also has limited empirical support (White, et al., 1986). Herzberg's theory, however, is easy to put into practice and is intuitively logical and has had a positive effect on business organizations.

According to Mayes (1978), "In examining the content of all three theories, most analyses of work motivation tend to support Alderfer's theory over Maslow's and Herzberg's" (pp. 51-52). Magnuson (1992) mentions, "It is believed that the ERG theory takes some of the strong points of the earlier content theories but is not as restrictive and limiting" (p. 29). The results of the studies of Magnuson (1992), Becker (1983) and Hoff (1988) have indicated, "The hygiene factors do not play a significant role in the decision of present employees" (p. 134). Seguin (1997) in his research study of motivation writes, "It is ironic that the only areas of the Maslow needs hierarchy and Herzberg's two-factor theory that produced significant results were from the two lower level needs" (p. 117). Leath (2000) has revealed in his research that "The highly involved employees may not always seek out higher level needs, but through their involvement and often the encouragement of others ... involvement allows employees to belong, to earn respect and influence, and to accomplish greatness in the face of adversity, challenge and risk" (p. 260).

In sum, many research studies reveal that Maslow's needs hierarchy and Herzberg's two-factor theory may not meet today's organizational requirements for motivating employees. Their theories are based on hierarchy and stages. Alderfer's ERG theory, on the other hand, continues to have favorable application in organizations but deserves further analysis (Magnuson, 1992). Alderfer ERG theory is a continuum process in oppose to staged-based process.

Organizations, administrators and policy makers may gain valuable knowledge and information in recognizing the impact of motivational theories such as those of Maslow, Herzberg and Alderfer and address job satisfaction, recognition programs, and growth opportunities.

Basis of Organizational Change

Introduction

Our world now seems defined more by chaos and change than by stability. It seems that change is overwhelming our ability to cope emotionally, to manage our affairs and to plan for our future. The impact of change on organizations in the past centuries was relatively isolated and cyclic, but now as organizations grow and evolve, they are continuously subjected to the influence of internal and external factors that lead to a need for change. According to Webster's dictionary (1988), the meaning of change is "to transform, alter, to convert" (p. 234).

The purpose of this section is to analyze leadership problems in managing organizational change, using Lewin's change model as the fundamental and theoretical model for organizational change, Hall's model as a tool, and Kubler-Ross's model as a path to prevent resistance to change. First, a review of each theory will be discussed. Second, advantages and disadvantages of the theories will be discussed. Finally, a summary of change management will be presented.

Lewin's Theory of Change Model

A theory that has been used as a model for implementing change in organizational settings is Lewin's theory of planned change (as cited in Hall, 1997). The three phases identified in Lewin's change process include "unfreezing, moving or changing and refreezing" (Lewin, 1947, p.34).

Lewin
Change Model

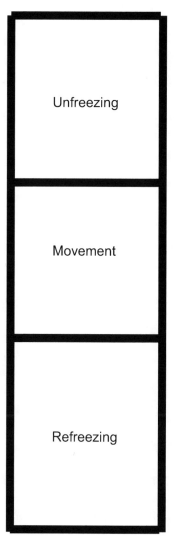

This model is used to assist the organization in overcoming obstacles and bringing about effective change. Roberts (1997) wrote, "Lewin was the early pioneer for change and transition study" (p. 234). Hayden (1998) writes, "Lewin conceived of change as modifying the forces that keep a system's behavior stable, thus at any time behavior is the result of forces striving to maintain the status quo and those pushing for change" (p. 30).

Morgan (1997) reveals that in Lewin's theory of change "any potential change is resisted by forces working in the opposite direction ... the idea is similar to the dialectical principle that everything generates its opposite" (p. 294). Unfreezing is the stage of preparing a situation for change and developing a felt need for change by showing discrepancies between current behaviors and desired future behaviors. According to Lewin (1958), in the unfreezing process "making the individual or organization uncomfortable enough with the old way that they would try to find something new" (p. 115). "In this phase the identification of a need for change and the establishment of a receptive climate" (Lewin, 1947, pp. 237-242).

Identifying factors that present potential obstacles to successful change, communicating information about the problem to all employees in the organization, and outlining the benefits associated with the new change are strategies for unfreezing the environment. In this case the employees are supportive of the proposed change, but the administration requires further convincing. Lewin (1947) writes, "When employees process social information as a collective intelligence, they compare the meaning of events in order to gain additional information about a change" (p. 41). Lewin sees conflict as an important unfreezing force in organizations.

The second stage involves taking the change from its original level to a new level, with the "implementation of new ideas, values, or behaviors that focus on the actual change" (Lewin, 1947, pp. 237-242). In the moving phase, change is actually implemented. This is the point at which changes in task, people, culture, technology, and structure are initiated. According to Wilson (1996), "Lewin's theory of change is necessary in order to develop steps to institute positive changes" (p. 35). Strategies in this phase involve applying specifics about the new policy, managing resistance to the change, and developing a written procedure for the change and a model for notifying employees when the change will take place. Lewin warns that if this phase of change is entered prematurely, and people are not ready for change, they will resist.

The third phase involves "refreezing new behavior patterns into place" (Lewin, 1947, pp. 237-242). In this phase, the concern is for stabilizing the change and creating the conditions for continuity. Lewin emphasis that refreezing is accomplished by providing appropriate awards for performance and positive reinforcement. Strategies used during this phase reinforce adoption of the change until it is integrated. Assessments, feedback and joint action planning are performed. When refreezing is done poorly, changes may be quickly forgotten or abandoned over time. When it is done well, change can be long lasting. "If one wants to understand a system, one should try to change it" (Lewin, 1944, pp.195-200).

Once a change has been accepted and implemented by an organization, the initiators of the change must keep working with the members and emphasizing the positive effects of the change. Otherwise, the organization may slowly lapse into its old habits. Lewin (1935) states, "The direction of the field force plays an important part in such intelligent behavior as it has to do with detour problems" (p. 82).

Kubler-Ross's Theory

A critical issue in change and managing change is dealing effectively with the emotions in organizational affairs. Kubler-Ross is one of the most important contributors to our understanding of the human response to stress and resistance to change. Kubler-Ross (1969) identifies five stages of human response to dramatic change: "1) denial and isolation, 2) anger, 3) bargaining, 4) depression and resignation and 5) acceptance" (p. 41).

According to Kubler-Ross (1969), "Denial is an outgrowth of the failure of most individuals to anticipate and thus begin to emotionally prepare for traumatic events in their lives" (p. 41-43). For most people, the idea of "it could never happen to me" all too quickly transforms into "it hasn't happened to me" when disaster actually occurs. Kubler-Ross (1969) writes, "Denial is usually accompanied by isolation from any part of the environment, which may tend to remind the individual that the traumatic change has in fact occurred" (p. 342). Denial and isolation are emotional protection for the individual and thus are often not principled or thoughtful opposition to the change, though they are often mistaken for being so. Kubler-Ross (1969) notes that this response "is analogous to the phenomenon of psychological flight, which is the tendency of individuals to flee danger" (p. 343). The alternative phenomenon, psychological flight, is analogous to the next Kubler-Ross stage.

Kubler-Ross (1969) explains, "Anger is a familiar but often misinterpreted response to traumatic change (...) as the veil of denial falls from the eyes of the individual, and the pain of the change begins to be felt, anger is an inevitable result" (p. 42). Feelings of unfair treatment, resentment about past injustices and an infinite array of other motivations serve to

fuel one's anger.

Kubler-Ross
Denial & Acceptance Model

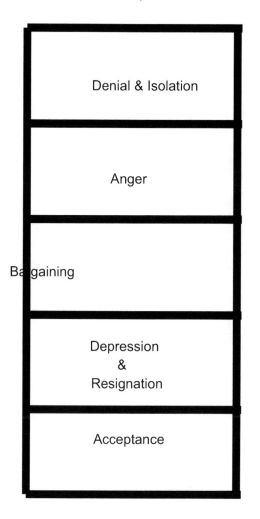

Kubler-Ross (1969) writes, "In contrast to the stage of

denial, this stage of anger is very difficult to cope with from the point of view of family and staff. The reason for this is the fact that this anger is displaced in all directions and projected onto the environment at times almost at random" (p. 64). Additionally, groups of people with such fears often find comfort in sharing their fears with one other, creating a "group" fear and thus making the change process more difficult. Kubler-Ross (1983) writes, "Fears are gifts to us since they preserve life (...) either knowingly or unconsciously, we pass our acquired fears along to our children and are not aware until it is too late that these cause indescribable damage and pain" (p. 61).

According to Kubler-Ross (1969), "when denial and anger fail to make the change disappear, the next resistance to change is bargaining" (p. 64). This period is an effort by the individual, in every way possible, to mitigate the impact of the change and to buy time. Kubler-Ross (1969) writes that to some extent "it is an extension of the tendency to deny the change (...) but here the denial is selective" (pp. 42-43). Individuals may accept parts of the change phenomenon and deny others. In this stage, the individual wants to make a deal between the change factors that seem to be inevitable and those that do not. Kubler-Ross (1969) writes, "The bargaining is really an attempt to postpone; it has to include a prize offered for good behavior; it also sets a self–imposed deadline" (p. 95).

"Depression is the final barrier to acceptance of change" (Kubler-Ross, 1969, p. 342). It may start with reaction or depression over what has been lost. Then it is anticipatory depression over what is expected to be lost. Resignation usually follows. "An understanding person will have no difficulty eliciting the cause of the depression and alleviating some of the unrealistic guilt or shame which often accompanies the depression" (Kubler-Ross, 1969, p. 98).

Kubler-Ross (1969) writes, "Acceptance is the final phase" (p. 43). In this stage rational action on the part of the individual usually begins. "Acceptance is not necessarily either happy or satisfied or unhappy and dissatisfied (...) what it is, is clear: the individual finally sees the truth and is dealing with it, effectively or not, as a reality" (Kubler-Ross, 1969, p. 43).

Hall's Theory

Hall (1997) writes, "A critical step in improving or changing any organization is diagnosing or analyzing its present functioning" (p. 255). Many change and organizational development efforts fall short of their objectives because this important step is not taken or is conducted superficially. Hall's theory is based on developing an understanding of how various change tools and strategies can be used to solve problems of an organization. According

to Anthony (1996), "To Hall and his associates, a planned

change within an organization includes a resource system to

support the planned change, time, materials and training" (p.

25). To understand Hall's organizational change theory is to

understand the effects of decision-making and resistance on

planned change programs that he has created. His model is

based on "governing values, action strategies and

consequences" (Hall, 1997, p. 385). Hall has created this

theory of change management to improve the ability of

managers and organizations to learn from their experience.

Hall's model begins with the underlying values on which

the theory is based. Hall (1997) writes, "These are the values

of unilaterally controlling the situation, maximizing the

probability that we will win, minimizing the expression of

negative feelings, and emphasizing rationality" (p. 385). Most

changes in organizations, according to Hall, (1997) are

"seldom confined to the technical aspects of production" (p. 267).

Hall asserted that employee self-reliance in "the new social contract requires an ability to develop meaningful relationships and master the art of being connected with others at all levels" (Hall, 1996, p. 103).

Hall
Change Model

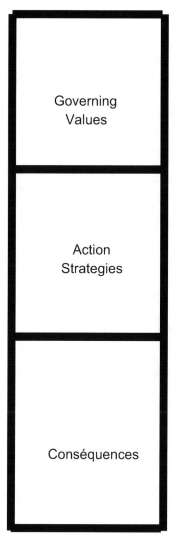

Governing
Values

Action
Strategies

Conséquences

Not   only   must   new   methods   of   change   in   an

organization be of high quality, workable and efficient, they must also be acceptable to the employees who will be working in the organization. Hall (1997) writes, "The acceptance part is a factor that makes the problem of introducing changes different from purely technical and non-technical problems of evaluating new equipment or procedures" (p. 267). The communications strategy is important in implementing a change. One way to implement the communication strategies is to get employees involved in the decision-making and keep them in the communication loop throughout the life of the project. Hall (1996) writes, "You should include people at the lowest possible level that is appropriate in the dialogue" (p. 17). Training is also a key to a successful change implementation.

Hall (1996) states, "One of the most common and serious mistakes made by both the administrators and leaders of a planned change process is to presume that once an innovation has been introduced and initial training has been completed that intended users will put the innovation into practice" (p. 33). Hall believes that change occurs on an individual basis and states "it is naïve to assume that everyone will see the innovation the same way at the same time (Hall, 1991, p. 23).

Hall describes individuals working in organizations that encourage task mastery as being part of the old culture and those seeking relational skill building as part of the new era. Hall (1979) writes, "The feeling, perceptions, motivations and attitudinal dynamics of individuals as they first become aware of an innovation, approach to use and gradually become confident in their use of the change" (p. 4). One of the most encouraging aspects of Hall's change model is the consequence of a successful change implementation. He believes that organizations should allocate rewards based on how well employees contribute to supporting change efforts

(Hall, 1987). Rewards system in Hall's view will give employees a reason to really care about the success of the change initiative and will give them the feel of more control and more accountable for what happens in the form of their rewards changing as their performance changes.

Compare and Contrast Theories

The theories of Lewin, Hall and Kubler-Ross show that there is no best way for an organization to make a change. Hall believes effective organizational change rests on interrelated factors such as "coordination, commitment and competencies". Hall (1997) writes, "Coordination of effort or teamwork gives an organization the benefit of using existing employee knowledge and understanding to discover quality, product and service development opportunities" (p. 268). Commitment, he wrote, "Is essential to bring about cooperation with and implementation of changes" (p. 268). He further continues, The development of new competencies such as knowledge of the organization as a whole and the development of analytical and interpersonal skills are required for employees to identify and solve problems as team members ... if any of these elements are missing, the change process will break down (P. 268).

Lewin, Kubler-Ross and Hall are among the theorists who have contributed models, which provide well-thought-out courses to manage organizational change. One of the disadvantages of Lewin's change model is that it, unlike Hall's and Kubler-Ross's models, "provides a more general than specific description of the process of change" (Dickens, 1998, pp. 44-62). In other words, Lewin theory does not give details about the unfreezing, moving and refreezing processes and offers a general framework. By contrast, Hall's model provides more "detailed descriptions of the activities that should occur to ensure successful implementation and overcome obstacles of change" (Dickens, 1998, pp. 44-62). In oppose to Lewin's model, Kubler-Ross model provides stages in managing change. There has also been other persistent criticism of the original Lewin studies. Miller (1951) and Bennett (1955) criticize Lewin for his "uncontrolled variables in the experiment" studies (Bennett, 1955, p. 251). One problem with Lewin's model is that his conception of forces impinge upon an individual ... while Lewin offered a general framework for understanding change processes, his system did not offer the complexity necessary to measure continuing interactions (Weisbord, 1989).

Smith and Gemmill (1993) empirically explore and tested the Lewin theory of change, and their findings support the notion that "groups encounter change as ongoing, rather than one time process" (pp. 553-581). Kuler-Ross model, in the other hand is phase-based model and one needs to go through the stages in order to manage the change. Krikorian (1997) concludes, "While it provided insight into Lewin's notion of forces as a self-organizing system, it nevertheless failed to fully incorporate communication" (p. 8). In contrast to Lewin's model, Hall's model is based on coordination and communication. Argyris (1957) criticized Lewin's model for the use of decisions of only peripheral interest to workers and suggested that the experimental conditions created ... were atypical.

One of the advantages of Lewin's change model is that it is a "processed-based model" (Dickens, 1998, p. 62). Marrow (1969) reveals that Lewin's model "proceeds in a spiral of steps each of which is composed of a circle of planning, action and fact-finding about the result of the action" (p. 206).

Hall's theory of organizational changes is similar to Lewin's theory. Hall's model was also criticized for omitting employees in some of the change processes. In other words, in Hall's model, employees have no role-play in some of the decision making and controlling the change. Gomberg (1957) attacks Hall's model of change for "its neglect of trade unions and conflict, since techniques did not change the basic power

relationships, nor challenge management's right to control"
(pp. 348-370).

Hall's organizational change theory may be similar to
Lewin's; but in contrast to Lewin's theory of change, Hall
(1996) stresses "emphasis on working with employees in
making the acceptable change" and believes that
"management can control solution and the change by
reserving decision making to itself" (pp. 17-33). Hall (1989)
writes, "Acceptance is inherently voluntary with the
employees and is not subject to the will of management" (p.
268). Hall's (1997) model tends to focus on a few facets of
change in organization: "shared responsibility team" (p. 172),
integrating talented people with diverse skills and often
conflicting personal styles and goals; "continuous
development of individual skills" (p. 172), involving on-the-job
development achieved through challenging, diverse tasks and
daily interactions with other people from whom the

organization can learn; and "determining and building a common vision" (p. 172), relying heavily on leadership behavior and the "leader's ability to create organizational excitement and empowerment, to inspire employees to become committed to an organization's mission and sense of purpose" (p. 172).

Lewin's model is similar to Hall's model in some respects but omits employee's involvement in many tactical decisions making. Hall emphasizes that management cannot just sit back and make decisions on making change. They should consult with employees who can reveal what resources are needed for change, what barriers need to be broken down, and what staffing may be required. According to Hall (1996), "The ability for individuals to build collaborative relationships is an essential ingredient for implementing organizational change" (p. 18). Lurie (2000) mentions that "Hall's work ... is based upon a relational approach for continuous learning and development (p. 32).

One of the advantages of Kubler-Ross's model is that it is easy to use and is built on stages and transitional steps. She argues, "People go through stages when confronted with a serious loss in their lives" (Kubler-Ross, 1983, p. 61). But she neglects to apply her theory of managing change to groups and organizational settings. Another disadvantage of her theory is that it omits the role of sponsorship. Kubler-Ross model is a particularly important one because it helps explain many of the otherwise confusing behaviors of people going through transition (Lurie, 2000). In oppose to Hall's and Lewin's model, Kubler-Ross theory helps individuals to guide the behavior of others who seek to respond effectively to the rigors of change.

In contrast to Hall's and Lewin's model, Kubler-Ross focuses on stages that are dramatic and affect human emotions. Her model may be used after the change is occurred (after the fact) rather than assisting individuals in making the change or leading the change. In many cases, employees consider organizational transformation as traumatic both operationally and individually. Bond (1998) mentions that "Kubler-Ross's predictable stages are windows into the behavior of individuals and groups undergoing the trauma of change" (p. 342). Similar to Hall's model, Kubler-Ross (1997) mentions that involvement is part of employee empowerment, which concentrates on pushing downward throughout an organization. In contrast to Lewin's model, Kubler-Ross believes that with empowerment, workers feel they are a valued part of the organization. Empowerment involves giving workers the knowledge, the tools, and the responsibility to improve work processes. Similar to Kubler-Ross's model, Hall's theory suggests that allowing and encouraging employee participation in a change program may result in a greater sense of psychological ownership that

subsequently may affect resistance to or promotion of the
change effort. Kubler-Ross argues that people go through
stages when confronted with a serious loss in their lives. She
explains, "Considerate managers should realize that these
stages exist and handle them when the change occurs in the
organizations" (Schweiger, Ivancevich, and Power, 1987, pp.
127-138).

Similar to Lewin's and Hall's model, Kubler-Ross
believes that resistance to change is a major problem in
making the change. Kubler-Ross (1969) states, "Resistance
is a process of conscious or unconscious blocking as a
means of seeking safety" (pp. 342-343). She believes that
"Anger is the next step in overcoming the change process"
(pp. 342-343). Many employees go through the bargaining
phase when denial and anger fail to make the change
disappear. Kubler-Ross (1969) writes, "The next stage of
resistance to change is bargaining, where employees try to

bargain their way into not accepting the change" (p. 65).

People tend to view organizational transition as essentially a traumatic period, and difficulties must be overcome every step of the way. Most of the time, "the obstacles and the resistance during transition are the greatest dangers to the success of the change effort" (Kubler-Ross, 1969, p. 342). But the transition period also involves emotional opportunity. "The excitement and euphoria associated with dramatic, positive change can be a significant motivational force and a major spur to creativity and innovation" (Kubler-Ross, 1969, p. 343). In similar to Hall's model, Kubler-Ross believes that these energies should not be ignored during the transition discussion, particularly if the entire team is present. The negative aspects of transition can be viewed as a protective emotional shell, the removal of which can liberate transition participants to find their positive, supportive motivations (Kubler-Ross, 1997).

Resistance is a process of conscious or unconscious blocking as a means to seeking safety (Kubler-Ross, 1997). Lewin believes that to over come the resistance one makes the individual uncomfortable enough with the old way that they would try to find something new. In contrast to Lewin's model Kubler-Ross believes that "in resistance stage the survival and well being of individuals are threatened". In this stage the most primitive of defense systems or resistance is activated. Kubler-Ross (1969) writes, "The most common form of resistance is denial" (p. 42). At the individual level, patterns of resistance to change are influenced by the magnitude of risk-taking - the potential loss of job, livelihood, material possession, or even death - associated with a particular change (Kubler-Ross, 1997). To overcome resistance one needs to provide empathy and support, encourage participation and involvement and communication adequate information (Kubler-Ross-1997). In contrast to

Lewin's model, Hall uses various anti resistance tools in order to over come the resistance. One Hall's tools is to involve employees in the change process right from the beginning. People who participate are far more likely to support the change that are imposed on individuals or organizations, even if the changes are conducive to one's well-being.

In contrast to Lewin's model, Hall's model supports individual involvement. Hall argues when people do not participate, then, they are likely to either subvert the change effort or minimize its effectiveness. Hayden (1998) reveals, "Lewin's model provides the fundamental, theoretical model for managing organizational change from which the other models are built and adapted" (p. 29). Hall's change management model is specified in detail and in step-by-step processes. Hall (1987) writes, "Attention is focused on the processes and tasks of using the innovation and the best use of information and resources" (p. 60). The change management of the Kubler-Ross model provides an explanation of the effect of change. In contrast to Hall's and Lewin's model, Kubler-Ross model is important because it helps to understand the levels of human behaviors thought transition and change implementation.

Lewin's model (as cited in Hall, 1997) is ideal for implementing change in an organization. While Kubler-Ross model is ideal for individuals. Lewin's (1947) change model has been shown to be "effective because it can be applied to any setting, is easy to follow, and incorporates strategies to identify and resolve obstacles during the change process" (pp. 87-95). Hall model of change is ideal for organizational setting and similar to Lewin's model is phases-based model. Hall model is very detailed and specific to the settings, Lewin's model, in contrast, is not very detailed and not so specific. The simplicity of Lewin's model seems appropriate, in some cases, because the proposed change model is relatively straightforward and affects a number of employees within the organization.

Lewin (1935) writes, "Direction [is] ... indicated by the fact that one cannot force a solution of the detour by increasing the strength of the valence ... if the attraction is much too weak, it is, to be sure, unfavorable" (p. 83). In other words, force of change needs to be such that it does not create resistance. Managing resistance in any organizational change is a difficult task. Lewin (1952) writes, "Organizations encounter resistance to change as they seek to shape their future" (p. 459). Hall (1997) believes, "People resist change simply because it is change" (p. 385). Kubler-Ross (1969) writes, "When the pain of the change bins to be felt, anger is an inevitable result" that may follow with resistance (p. 64).

Hall (1987) contends that changing worker behavior is like "skinning cats" and may be approached in a variety of ways. "How it is approached will depend on the nature of the underlying problem" (p. 272). Hall believes that by applying and implementing a problem-solving strategy an organization can overcome resistance and accomplish a successful organizational change. Hall (1986) writes, "Analyze the problem ... develop a change strategy, and select a method for implementing that strategy" (p. 273).

In addition to overcoming resistance to change, Lewin (1958) explains "Managing change is concerned with many other aspects of moving the structure, processes and culture from an old condition to a new one, and sustaining change" (p. 115). Hall (1997), on the other hand, argues that to introduce change, an organization should be engaged in "selling and mutual problem solving" (p. 268). In selling, Hall means the facts and arguments are presented to employees showing the advantages of change and in mutual problem solving. Hall also believes that managers should discuss with their subordinates the need for change, soliciting their ideas, and then make the decision. In contrast to Lewin's theory, Hall's model provides ways to make change through consultation with employees and subordinates. Hall (1997) writes, "In order to deal with problem of change, the first step is to learn the nature of the resistance to change ... once the nature of the resistance is defined, change process can be implemented successfully" (p. 268).

Vitucci (1996) uses the analogy of an ice cube to explain the change process of Lewin's change model. He writes, "The ice cube in its original shape represents the current state of the organization. In order to change, the ice cube must be unfrozen, molded to its new shape, and then, refrozen" (p. 56). Similarly, the organization, in order to change positively, must melt any forces that resist change and "create a climate of acceptance and trust that will reinforce or refreeze the new state of the organization"

(Lewin, 1951, pp. 228-229). Several sources cite Lewin's change model as an effective framework for instituting planned organizational change (Hall, 1997). In Lewin's change management model, he conceived of change as "modifying the forces that keep a system's behavior stable, thus at any time behavior is the result of forces striving to maintain the status quo and those pushing for change" (Lewin, 1947, pp. 87-95). "When both forces are equal", he believes, "behavior is maintained in a state of quasi-stationary equilibrium" (Lewin, 1947, pp. 87-95). To change that state, one must increase or decrease those forces in some combination otherwise, it may cause a great deal of conflict.

Lewin sees conflict as an important unfreezing force in organizations. Lewin (1936) writes, "Conflict helps people break old habits and recognize alternative ways of thinking about or doing things" (p. 41). Resolving conflicts may help in making a smooth transitional change. Hall (1979) writes, "The conflict is often accompanied by stress and in extreme cases, even health problems occur (...) one way to reduce these conflicts is through managing our roles" (p. 471). In contrast to Kubler-Ross model, Lewin's model of change is generally recognized as the "underlying and guiding frame of reference for any organization development effort" (Lewin, 1952, p. 473).

Organizational change to Hall's (1979) view is "to developing a new mission, a new vision, a fresh image of the future is the process of creating a desired state (...) that is more desirable than the present state" (p. 115). Lewin (1951) states, "The unfreezing of the present level may involve quite different problems in different cases (...) to break open the shell of complacency and self-righteousness it is sometimes necessary to bring about deliberately an emotional stir-up" (pp. 228-229). In Kubler-Ross model, a critical issue in organizational change is dealing effectively with the difficult and emotional transition from the present state to the future. Hall's and Lewin's models do not deal with the difficult parts of emotional transitions that individuals go through and that is a major difference between Hall's and Lewin's model to Kubler-Ross's model in making an organizational change.

In Hall's view organizational change that is planned and managed by internal people can be successful and goal-oriented. Hall mentions that employees should learn and apply the principles about how to master and manipulate the forces of change to achieve their intended goals. Lewin (1951) writes, "The question of planned change is identical with the question: what conditions have to be changed to bring about a given result and how can one change these conditions with the means at hand?" (p. 172). Lewin (1947) writes, "The original formulation of action consists of analysis, fact-finding, conceptualization, planning, execution, more fact-finding or evaluation and then a repetition of this whole circle of activities" (p.4).

Once change is introduced, the direction and magnitude of the organization's course of change is altered over time in such a way as to counteract the effects of productivity and fall below the expected results. Lewin (1958) writes, If we cannot judge whether an action had led forward or backward, if we have no criteria for evaluating the relation between effort and achievement, there is nothing to prevent us from making the wrong conclusions and to encourage the wrong work habits (p. 115).

Some of the tools that may help in managing organizational change are technology, communication, teamwork, and employees' involvement. The guiding principle is that both leadership and employees must listen as carefully as they speak in order to have any chance of understanding each other. Hall (1997b) advises, "Communicate issues associated with the key areas of change to all employees" (p. 385). With the use of a single computerized information system, vast amounts of information can be aggregated and used to make decisions centrally. Hall (1997a) suggests, "Create a team that can help managing change" (p. 237). The literature suggests that implementation of a change is most likely to occur in an environment that supports collaboration, collegiality, chaos and diversity.

The ability to effectively generate, acquire and use knowledge is important for many employees to remain vital in today's organizations when they go through the change process. The leaders of the organization must be at the forefront of change. The change process requires a shift in organizational attitudes. Lewin (1936) writes, "In dealing with change it is often a question not of comparing any given situation with each other, but rather of determining changes of situation" (p. 159).

As it was mentioned before some believe that to over come the resistance one makes the individual uncomfortable enough with the old way that they would try to find something new. Enlisting the closer involvement of employees in business operations and their support in organizational support entails a carefully "planned communications strategy" (Hall, 1997b, p. 385) which relies on a comprehensive grasp of how people deal with change in their lives. Hall (1997a) writes, "Effective communication is a two-way process, so business enterprises must also listen and be prepared to deal with what they hear" (p. 268). By focusing on the collective goal of the organization, the organization can adapt to the changing environment and effectively sustain the functions necessary for continued survival.

Organization Change Conclusion

From the literatures that were reviewed one can see that sustaining an organizational change is a complicated and time-consuming task. All three organizational change models are based on one fundamental insight - which major change will not happen easily for a long list of reasons. Hall et al. (1997) conclude that to be effective, a method must be designed to alter strategies, reengineer processes or improve quality that addresses barriers of change and addresses them well. Others believe the change should occur from the top to the down – a top-down model. The steps or layers of change should occur without a gap or disparity between the current level and desired level of performance in the organization. The level of change should be identified and should not be large enough to hurt the organization. In this case the status quo is disturbed when the organization recognizes that the distance between where they are (the existing level) and where they want to be (the desired level) must be reduced. Such awareness in Lewin's model literally unfreezes the system from establishing behaviors, attitudes, and policies and prepares it for adaptation and innovation. Lewin (1952) states that some of the change processes "help defrost a hardened status quo ... if change was easy, you would not need all that effort" (pp. 459-473).

Kubler-Ross (1969) mentions there are many ways in "making the organization transformation and overcoming the emotional transition" (p. 342). Kubler-Ross's model is geared toward dealing with change when the actual change is occurred. For the most part this may be dealing with emotional and psychological transition rather than dealing with the actual change process.

In sum, the purpose of change is to affect the knowledge, values, attitudes, and beliefs of the people within the organization. The logical outcome should be a change in behavior. Two basic lessons underscored by all implementation models reviewed here are: (a) the change process typically occurs in multiple steps or layers that take a considerable amount of time to unfold, and efforts to bypass steps seldom yield a satisfactory result, and (b) mistakes in any step can slow implementation, as well as negate hard-won progress. Both lessons are valuable for all those involved in understanding and implementing change.

Social Aspects of Change

To understand any phenomenon as complex as social change, we need the systematic, conscious, and deliberate process of theory building. We also need theoretical perspectives in order to give coherence and rationality to social praxis. This section consists of inquiries into the dynamics of social change, as they are unraveled in the prodigious works of Arnold Toynbee, Auguste Comte, and Herbert Spencer.

This section first reviews the social change theories of Toynbee, Comte and Spencer separately and compares and contrasts their theories. We refer to work environment as a social place for employees to perform tasks and activities. In order to make a change to a work place one need to evaluate the dynamics of social change and the theories behind them. Furthermore, the human nature and human impact on the social order and the element of change as it relates to social change will be discussed.

Spencer's Theory of Social Change

Spencer's direct remark to social change was to unify the totality of human knowledge around the principle of evolution. Spencer builds a theory of change in which society is an organism. He uses his knowledge of biology to understand social phenomena. He believes that social change occurs as a result of physical, emotional and intellectual changes in individuals. Spencer believes the rate of change is limited by the rate at which individual change and pass on those individual modifications to succeeding generations. Spencer (1988) writes, "Environmental changes create new needs, new needs require new habits, which, in turn, require changes in the physical, emotional and intellectual traits of individuals ... these changed individuals then mold social institutions into corresponding forms" (P. 121).

The extent to which Spencer used biological ideas may be seen in his description of social institutions, which he spoke of in terms of sustaining, distributing, and regulating systems. Spencer (1969) writes, "The parts carrying on alimentation in a living body and the parts carrying on productive industries in the body politic, constitute, in either case, a sustaining system" (p. 58). In his view societal growth involves not only the multiplication of groups and the union of groups, but also increasing density or solidarity. The integration that follows differentiation means not merely a larger mass, but also the "progress of such mass toward that coherence due to closeness of parts" (p. 29).

It is clear that the evolutionary principle that Spencer found in the universe as a whole - indefinite, incoherent homogeneity giving way to a definite coherent heterogeneity - is also true of human societies. Spencer illustrates the societal transition from homogeneity to heterogeneity by contrasting primitive and modern societies. Spencer (1988) refers to the primitive tribe as "alike in all its parts" while the civilized nation is "full of structural and functional unlikeness" (p. 154). One can see that with increasing heterogeneity goes increasing coherence. The tribe, which Spencer is referring to, has more coherence for it is held together by subordination to the leader. This coherence increases until one achieves the civilized nation, which is sufficiently integrated to hold together for a thousand years.

Comte's Theory of Social Change

Comte has been identified as the father of sociology.

Simpson (1969) named him Sire of Sociology. Comte's own work was primarily not that of the innovator as much as that of the systematizer. He gathered together much of the thought of certain French thinkers, mixed it into a system and christened it sociology. Comte divides sociology into statics and dynamics. He refers to statical aspects of sociology as similar to what one would call structure, while dynamical aspects refer to change. Comte (1858) writes, "Statical sociology rests on the philosophical assumption that society is an organism united by consensus for there must always be a spontaneous harmony between the whole and the parts of the social system" (p. 461).

Comte believes that dynamical sociology is the study of the sequence of human development, and each step in that sequence is the necessary consequence of the preceding step. Comte (1858) identifies three stages of historical development that correspond to three stages of development in the human mind, "the theological, the metaphysical and the scientific" (p. 25). He believes that these three stages are both three successive methods of intellectual functioning and three corresponding types of social orders. He emphasizes that in the theological state, intellectual functioning "supposes all phenomena to be produced by the immediate action of supernatural beings" (p. 26). Comte subdivides the theological state into three stages: fetishism, polytheism and monotheism. The stage of fetishism marked the beginning of the theological era of humankind. In this stage Comte (1858) states that man "conceives of all external bodies as animated by a life analogous to his own, with differences of mere intensity" (p. 545). In the state of fetishism, society was characterized by sacerdotal authority, by the beginning of the conquest of nature and by behavior based more on affect than on the intellect.

It is certain that Comte views change in terms of

progress. He sees progress as occurring in every facet of the social order, including the physical, ethical, intellectual and political realms. Comte's thought has been well summarized by Aron (1968) that writes, "According to Comte social disorders were rooted in the simultaneous existence of three incompatible philosophies: "theological, metaphysical and positive" (p. 36). Any of the three, he believes, can create a social order, but their coexistence precludes any sort of order. Comte (1858) writes, It is only through the more and more marked influence of the reason over the general conduct of man and of society, that the gradual march of our race has attained that regularity and persevering continuity which distinguish it so radically from the desultory and barren expansion of even the highest of the animal orders, which share, and with enhanced strength, the appetites, the passions, and even the sentiments of man (p. 521).

One can see that the social order that could be created

by the positive mind is one of intellectual and moral progress toward benevolence among fellow humans.

Toynbee's Theory of Social Change

According to Lauer (1990) "Toynbee defines, six civilizations that arose spontaneously from primitive societies ... the Egyptian, the Sumerian, the Chinese, the Mayan, the Minoan, and the Indic" (p. 40). Lauer (1990) in his research about Toynbee social change theory notes that "each of these (civilizations) arose independently of the others, and they appeared in widely separated areas ... all other civilizations derive from these original six" (pp. 40-41). Toynbee (1957) first examines racial and environmental explanations and rejects them. He explains that the "Egyptian civilization arose as the result of an adequate response to the challenge of the swamps and jungles of the Nile Valley, while other civilizations emerged from the challenge of inter-group conflict" (pp. 41-42). Toynbee (1957) refers to five different stimuli. "Hard countries, new ground, blows, pressures, and penalizations" (pp. 88-139). He refers to "hard countries as a difficult physical environment", such as living by a river. New ground refers to "land that has not been settled and tilled". Toynbee (1957) refers to blows as "sudden military defeats" (p. 88), while pressures indicate a situation of continuing external threat. Penalizations refer to those classes and races that have historically been subjected to various forms of oppression, discrimination and exploitation.

Toynbee (1961) writes, "All acts of social creation are the work either of individual creators or at most of creative minorities" (p. 214). In his view the task of the minority is not simply to create new social forms and processes, but to "contrive some means of carrying this sluggish rear-guard along with them in their eager advance" (p. 215). Toynbee (1957) calls the civilization growth a process of "etherialization, a shift of emphasis from some lower sphere of being or of action to higher" (p. 198). Toynbee was concerned about the prospects of Western civilization as well as the fate of past civilizations. He suggests a number of basic problems that would have to be confronted and somehow resolved problems that are as pressing today as they were many years ago when Toynbee wrote about them. One is the problem of war, which was a primary cause of the breakdown and disintegration of civilizations of the past. A second problem is that of class conflict.

Industrialization means that the bulk of material goods need no longer be monopolized by a privileged few. People will no longer be content unless they are free from want. Somervell (1961) in his study of Toybee's system writes, It looked as if the regimentation imposed by industrial technology might be taking the life out of the pre-industrial spirit of private enterprise, and this prospect opened up a further question. Would the technical system of mechanized industry be able to survive the social system of private enterprise? And, if not, would the Western civilization itself be able to survive the death of a mechanized industry, to which it had given hostages by allowing its population to increase in the machine age far beyond the numbers that any non-industrial economy could support (p. 338).

Third basic problem identified by Toynbee is "population growth". "If that can be solved", he said, "we would need to address the problem of leisure" (p. 256). All of these problems remain crucial to human well being. Toynbee draws for us of the history of humankind is one of continuing cycles of birth, growth, breakdown and disintegration of civilizations. Toynbee sees this whole process as being intimately tied up with the functioning of elite and their relationships with the masses, both the internal and external proletariats.

Compare and Contrast Theories

Comte and Toynbee were afraid of an increase in population. Lauer (1990) writes, "Comte referred not simply to more numbers but to density of population ... the higher concentration of human in a given space will create new wants and new problems, and therefore generate new means of progress" (p. 60). It was Comte (1858) who first coined the expression "sociology". Comte's positive philosophy emanated from his historical study of the progress and "development of the human mind" (Comte, 1858, p. 25). His sole interest, however, was the western European mind and by mind, he meant the sciences, especially astronomy, physics, chemistry and biology. Comte believed that historical development revealed a matching movement of ideas and institutions. In the "course of positive philosophy" (Comte,

1858, p. 36), Comte attempted to demonstrate that each science is necessarily dependent on the previous science, that is, science can only be understood historically as the process of greater perfection. Although Spencer seems to have protested too much in disclaiming any profound influence of Comte's thought on his own, it might be true that his general orientation differs significantly from Comte's. Spencer (1894) described their different approaches in this way, What is Comte's professed aim? To give a coherent account of the progress of human conceptions. What is my aim? To give a coherent account of the progress of the external world. Comte proposes to describe the necessary, and the actual, filiations of ideas. I propose to describe the necessary, and the actual, filiations of things. Comte professes to interpret the genesis of our knowledge of nature. My aim is to interpret ... the genesis of the phenomena, which constitute nature, the one is subjective. The other is objective.

Comte was not only interested in the development of ideas but also in the correlative changes in social organization, and he dealt with social order as well as with progress. Nevertheless, Spencer correctly perceived the essential differences between them. Spencer's first and foremost concern was with evolutionary changes in social structures and social institutions rather than with the attendant mental states. Elworthy (1999) writes, "Spencer's eminence came from his ability to transform diverse facts and sciences of the modern world into one law of evaluation from incoherent homogeneity to coherent heterogeneity" (p. 22). Spencer argued, that the evolution of human societies, far from being different from other evolutionary phenomena, is but a special case of a universally applicable natural law.

It is axiomatic to Spencer that ultimately all aspects of the universe, whether organic or inorganic, social or nonsocial, are subject to the laws and "the principle of evolution ... a passage from an indefinite, incoherent homogeneity to a definite, coherent heterogeneity" (p. 667). In contrast, Somervell (1961) writes, "Toynbee believes that no civilization continues to grow indefinitely and there is a breakdown, which occurs when the creative elite no longer functions adequately, the majority no longer gives its allegiance to and imitates the elite, and social unity disintegrates" (p. 407). He mentions that Egyptian society continued as an identifiable civilization, but it was stagnant as far as cultural production was concerned. He further writes, "Like an individual, who has lost virtually everything but the capacity to breathe and eat and cling to life, Egyptian society lingered on but contributed nothing of value" (Somervell, 1961, p. 407).

Spencer proposed another basis for distinguishing between types of societies. To distinguish between what he called militant and industrial societies, Spencer used as the basis a difference in social organization brought about through forms of social regulation. This classification is at variance with that based on stages of evolution. Spencer (1851) writes, The trait characterizing the militant structure throughout is that its units are coerced into their various combined actions. As the soldier's will is so suspended that he becomes in everything the agent of his officer's will, so is the will of the citizen in all transactions, private and public, overruled by that of the government. The cooperation by which the life of the militant society is maintained is compulsory cooperation ... just as in the individual organism the outer organs are completely subject to the chief nervous center (pp. 19-23).

The industrial type of society, in contrast, is based on voluntary cooperation and individual self-restrain. Spencer (1955) writes,

Characterized throughout by the same individual

freedom, which every commercial transaction implies. The cooperation by which the multiform activities of the society are carried on becomes a voluntary cooperation. And while the developed sustaining system which give to a social organism the industrial type acquires for itself, like the developed sustaining system of an animal, a regulating apparatus of a diffused and un-centralized kind, it tends also to decentralize the primary regulating apparatus by making it derive from numerous classes its disputed powers (pp. 500-502).

Spencer stressed that the degree of societal complexity is independent of the militant-industrial dichotomy. Relatively undifferentiated societies may be "industrial" in Spencer's sense, and modern complex societies may be militant. What determines whether a society is militant or industrial is not the level of complexity but rather the presence or absence of conflict with the outside (McClellan, 1999).

Spencer was not the optimist that Comte and Toynbee were, however, unlike others he saw the possibility of societal regression as well as progress. Spencer (1969) writes, "If the general direction of evolution is toward the industrial society, it should be noted that it is possible to revert back to a more militant society" (p. 664). The role of sociology is to identify the process and help people to accept it and calmly await the appearance of the new age. Spencer (1874) writes, "See how comparatively little can be done and yet to find it worth while to do that little, so uniting philanthropic energy with philosophic calm" (p. 404). Spencer ideal society is one in which individuals may freely pursue their own interests. Spencer cherished the autonomy of the individual while at the same time he affirmed the inexorable process of development that transcends the individual.

One example, Spencer argues, is that "great

civilizations can only arise in temperate zones...emerged out of the bloody throes of societal wars" (p. 178). Toynbee's difference is that he says adverse conditions cause civilizations to arise. Somervell (1961) writes, "Toynbee recognizes five different stimuli: hard countries, new ground, sudden military defeats, pressures and penalizations such as classes and races subjected to oppression, discrimination and exploitation" (p. 49).

Spencer believed that a prime motivating factor in human beings coming together was the threat of violence and war. Spencer saw human life on a continuum with, but also as the culmination of, a lengthy process of evolution, and he held that "human society reflects the same evolutionary principles as biological organisms do in their development" (Lauer, 1990, p. 62). Society he believed, function without external control, just as the digestive system or a lower organism does (though, in arguing this, Spencer failed to see the fundamental differences between "higher" and "lower" levels of social organization). For Spencer, all natural and social development reflected on knowledge and intellectual abilities and the universality of law. Spencer (1938) writes, "Knowledge of the lowest kind is unified knowledge" (p. 442).

If we look at the linear developmental theories of Comte and Spencer it becomes cloudier. Comte seemed to think that society was progressing toward a more humane social order. Spencer theorized toward a utopian future similar to Comte's but saw the possible regressions that society might make as it progresses. Spencer, unlike Comte, thought that society guided itself in this progression and men had little influence over it.

The similarities in Toynbee, Comte and Spencer are that they all see the beginning, the growth, and stagnation leading to the end of societies. Jones (1997) in his research revealed that Comte refers to the nature of the human mind as the observation of the past that reveal the future. They each see different ends and different perspectives causing the changes. One can agree with Toynbee, in that he concerns himself with social-psychological aspects of change. All societies make change when change is inevitable, and rarely do they make changes when they are comfortable. Comte (1858) stated, "Man would not be happy without all of his faculties engaged. Man is an animal that must be stimulated or he will disintegrate" (p. 517). All civilizations seem to put forth their best efforts when challenged, and to stagnate when times are good. It is only when there are strong injustices that the people will want change, and then only if they have been forced into it.

All three theorists, Toynbee, Spencer and Comte, believed in studying aspects of history, stages or psychosocial processes to explain changes in society. All agree on stages or cyclic patterns of social change. All theorists believe that social change occurs as a result of physical, emotional and intellectual changes in individuals. Spencer saw progress in stages or events. He also agreed on the inevitability of the ultimate failure of a social system. McClellan (1999) writes, "Comte's view is that intellectual development is a social process that is reflected in the growth of knowledge and recapitulated in individuals through education and enculturation" (p. 365).

Agreeing that change is normal, Comte, Spencer and Toynbee find a structure-intellectual interaction philosophy in the context of change. These theorists believe that structure and intellect continuously impact the developmental progress of society. McClellan (1999) reveals, "Comte developed his philosophy of science by carrying on an early modern and enlightenment tradition of concern with the social organization of inquiry and the progress of knowledge" (p. 2).

Comte (1858) stated, "Man would not be happy without all of his faculties engaged" (pp. 25-26). Comte's vision of the future does not differ from that of Spencer and Toynbee. Comte (1848) writes, "Our characteristic qualities will find their most perfect respective confirmation, their most complete mutual harmony and the freest expansion for each and all" (p. 838). Comte goes beyond asking about the direction of change and inquires into the rate. There are three factors, according to Comte, that influence the rate of progress. The first is dissatisfaction. Comte (1858) writes, "Man, like other animals, can not be happy without a sufficient exercise of all his faculties, intense and persistent in proportion to the intrinsic activities of each faculty" (P. 517). Like modern self-actualization theorists, Comte saw a hierarchy of needs in humans, once their lower faculties have been exercised, they will be driven to use the higher. The greater the exercise of the higher faculties, the greater the rate of progress.

A second factor-affecting rate is the duration of human life. Comte (1969) writes, "An ephemeral life would be quite as mischievous as a too protracted one, by giving too much power to the instinct of innovation" (pp. 518-519). There is an optimum length of human life for an optimum rate of progress and any increase or decrease in average life span will affect that rate to some degree.

The third factor-affecting rate of change is the demographic one. The natural increase of population. This contributes more than any other factor to the acceleration of progress. Comte (1969) refers to this increase not simply to more numbers but to "density of population" (p. 518). The higher concentration of humans in a given space will create new wants and new problems and will therefore generate new means of progress and other "by neutralizing physical inequalities and affording a growing ascendancy to those intellectual and more forces which are suppressed among a scanty population" (Comte, 1969, p. 520). Comte was aware that factors influencing the rate of change can be extreme in two directions, not only can too slow a rate of population increase impede progress but too rapid a rate will do so as well by making the support of human life too difficult and the stability of social phenomena too fragile.

Toynbee focused on the processes of change, including birth, death, stagnation and disintegration. Toynbee predicts the decay and stagnation of Western cultures. Lauer (1990) writes, "Toynbee was concerned about the prospects of Western civilization as well as the fate of past civilizations" (p. 44). All three theorists were exceptional in developing insightful and dynamic social change stages and theories. Agreeing that change is normal, Comte and Spencer find a structure-intellectual interaction philosophy in the context of change. The theorists believe that structure and intellect continuously impact the developmental progress of society, but it is undetermined as to which had the most influence. Rafferty (1999) in his research study finds that Spencer was interested in "character not the knowledge of individuals". Spencer (1883) writes, "I regard social progress as mainly a question of character and not the knowledge or enlightenment ... the inherited and organized natures of individuals, only little modifiable in the life of a generation, essentially determine for the time being the type of social organization" (p. 171). They also find a relationship between direction and rate of change in the development of societies, the rate being affected by individual human factors.

In essence, the differences between the three theorists are in the analogies and relationships they use to relate their theory to social order development and their feelings about positive outcomes. Comte uses an analogy of society as an organism united by consensus. Unlike Spencer, he saw continuous positive progress occurring in every part of the social makeup, including the physical, ethical, intellectual and political realms. Soleiman-Panah (1999) writes, "In his System of Positive Philosophy, Comte lays out the epistemological foundation of sociology as the last positive science" (p. 36). Spencer believed society could regress as well as progress. Unlike Comte, he felt that there is probably an inverse relationship between the growth of culture and human happiness, and he does not buy into the fallacy of utopia apprehended.

Toynbee builds on Khaldun's concepts that "Humans are social creatures" (p. 45), carrying his theories out to encompass all of civilization, looking at the natural cycles of past civilizations as a way of understanding and explaining the collaborative nature of "individuals birth, growth, stagnation and disintegration in social life" (Toynbee, 1961, p.

198). Toynbee tells us that the history of humankind is one of continuing cycles of birth, growth, breakdown and disintegration of civilizations. Lauer (1990) writes, "Toynbee believes, the history of humankind is intimately tied up with the functioning of the elite and their relationships with the masses, both the internal and external proletariats" (pp. 41-44). Toynbee's civilization theories were criticized by Sorokin (1947), who says, "The theories have very little scientific use" (p. 87). Sorokin (1947) noted, "There are both quantitative and qualitative aspects to the growth and decline of a socio-cultural system" (p. 87).

The social theories of Spencer, Comte and Toynbee can be applied to organizational change. Spencer (1874) writes, "Social change occurs as a result of change, therefore, is limited by the rate at which individuals change and pass on those individual modifications to succeeding generations" (pp. 401-404). Organizational change, in

essence, create new needs; new needs require new ideas
which in turn require changes in the physical, emotional and
intellectual traits of individuals. Spencer sees the problem of
knowledge in modern science as a problem with the
development of science and developing conceptual system
and intellectual human labors. Spencer (1892) maintained
that there was a natural mechanism - an "innate moral sense"
- in human beings by which they come to arrive at certain
moral intuitions and from which laws of conduct might be
deduced" (p. 26). Thus one might say that Spencer held a
kind of "moral sense theory" (pp. 19-23). Spencer believes a
manifestation of his general idea of the persistence of force.
As this persistence of force was a principle of nature, and
could not be created artificially, Spencer held that no state or
government could promote moral feeling any more than it
could promote the existence of physical force. But while
Spencer insisted that freedom was the power to do what one
desired, he also held that what one desired and willed was

wholly determined by "an infinitude of previous experiences"

(Spencer, 1955, pp. 500-502).

Social Change Conclusion

Theorists such as Toynbee, Comte and Spencer have developed several ideas from which one can draw a picture of human nature and social change. Depending from which extremes of the spectrum a person selects his ideas, there could be broad social ramifications. Movement and change are essential features of any culture.

Spencer (1874) writes, "Society is an aggregate of individuals, and change in society could take place only once the individual members of that society had changed and developed (pp. 366-367). Individuals are, therefore, "primary", individual development was "egoistic" and associations with others largely instrumental and contractual.

The basic concept of change being a stimulus for

progress but also accounting for regression is an idea that parallels the writer's view. Looking at individuals' involvement in the change process seems to be out of balance in Spencer's theory. Nevertheless he accounts for the importance of the individual in the development of change. McClellan (1999) writes, "It is simply an attempt to clarify the social properties of the basic elements of society ... given an innate social sentiment or cooperative instinct, intellectual commerce is a natural result of human collaborating in the satisfaction of their common needs" (p. 398). Spencer accounts for multiple outcomes based upon how the information is channeled or acted upon. The similarities of the three theorists' Comte, Spencer and Toynbee contentions can be described as progressive, in terms of differentiation and integration on a continuum rather than a cyclical process. Their theories basically present social order development as an evolutionary or emergent process, new development coming from prior development in some manner.

One may argue that change is an unyielding process that moves in the direction of time. Things universally disintegrate and integrate in an endless cycle of change. Life forms revive and die. Change in its natural manifestation is neutral and free from value judgment. The human mind has an innate capacity for structured development (Piaget and Rolanda, 1989). Change relies on education, however, as we make a conscious and deliberate decision on how to respond to the ever present struggle between patterns of integration and disintegration in life. In every pattern of change, both "resistance" and "constructive accommodation to change" are discernable. It depends on how the event is interpreted and given a historical or phenomenological context.

In sum, education is truly the key element in initiating individual change and social progress. The question is what kind of education/learning/knowledge is necessary for individual and collective change? General education? Physical education? Physical sciences? Social sciences? Philosophy? Religion and ethics? It seems, however, that if education intends to become an agent of constructive, transformative change, some sort of evolving social consciousness should permeate the aim and content of education. McClellan (1999) in his research of social evolution writes, "Comte sees the problem of knowledge in modern science as a problem with the historical development of science when viewed as a developed conceptual system and as the result of combined human labors" (pp. 461-462).

The change process begins with the "individual" as the fundamental unit of change. Next is a social interaction. Human beings are social creatures. Any social phenomenon is the result of a meaningful "interaction" between two or more individuals. Interaction is necessary not only for material survival, but also for the emergence of meanings and values that comprises the non-material aspects of human life. It is through interaction that one may practice honesty or experience compassion. When a group of interacting individuals find some kind of group solidarity and cohesion, they form an "organization". To make a change one needs to be motivated to make efforts to change as individual. Individual effort in a group or an organization will create a sense of need to make a change as a group. Group efforts to make the change will cause the social change. It is a top down process that starts with individuals and ends at social level.

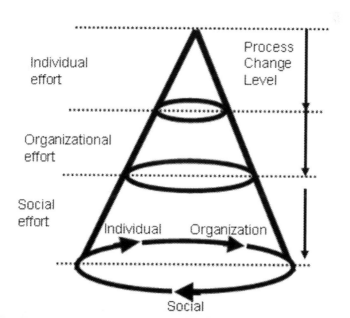

Top-Down Change Process

REFERENCES

Alderfer, C. P. (1969). An empirical test of a new theory of human needs. Organizational behavior and Human Performance, 4, 142-175.

Alderfer, C. P. (1972). Existence, relatedness and growth: Human needs in organizational setting. New York: Free Press.

Alderfer, C. P. (1973). A new design for survey feedback. Education Urban Society, 5, 437-464.

Alderfer, C. P. (1975). Learning from changing: Organizational diagnosis and development. Beverly Hills: Sage Publications, 510-511.

Alderfer, C. P. (1977). Organization development. Annual Review of Psychology, 28, 197-223.

Alderfer, C. P. (1989). Theories reflecting my personal experience and life development. The Journal of Applied Behavioral Science, 25, 351-365.

Alderfer, C.P. (1974). The effect of variations in relatedness need satisfaction on relatedness desires, 507.

Angielczky, C. (1997). Physician assistant satisfaction. Buffalo, NY: D'Youville College.

Anthony, L. D. (1996). A case study of conditions of planned change in organizations at the post implementation phase of electronic mail implementation. Detroit, Michigan: Graduate School of Wayne, 25.

Argyris, C. (1957). Personality and organization. New York: Harper.

Aron, R. (1968). Main currents in sociological thought. New York: Dover, 36.

Becker, W. A. (1983). A study of job satisfaction among returning camp counselors, Unpublished doctoral dissertation. Temple University, Philadelphia.

Bennett, B. E. (1951). Discussion, decision, commitment and

consensus in-group decision. Human Relations, 251-274.

Bond, V. (1998). Creating strategy. New York: Harper Collins, 28, 341-342.

Bowen, B. E. (1980). Job satisfaction of teacher educators in agriculture. Paper presented at Manitoba; Agriculture Education Research Meeting. Canada. March 5. Dialog, Eric text-fiche ED197060.

Bridges, W. (1994). Job shift: How to prosper in a workplace without jobs. Reading, Mass: Perseus Books, 202.

Brod, C. (1984). Techno-stress: The human cost of the computer revolution. Reading: MA: Addison-Wesley Publication, 43.

Bucklow, M. (1966). A new role for the work group. Journal of Applied Behavioral Science.

Callebaut, W. (1993). Taking the naturalistic turn or how real philosophy of science is done. Chicago: The University of Chicago Press, 445.

Chen, K. C. M. (1997). Motivation of Chinese printers in southern California. La Verne, California: University of La Verne Press.

Comte, A. (1848). Principles of sociology. New York: Calvin Blanchard, 838.

Comte, A. (1858). The positive philosophy, trans. Harriet Martineau. New York: Calvin Blanchard, 25-26.

Comte, A. (1969). Sociology. New York: Thomas Y. Crowell Co., 518.

Comte, A. (1974). Consideraions on the spiritual power. In Ronald Fletcher (ed.). The Crisis of Industrial Civilization: The Early Essays of Auguste Comte. London: Heinemann Educational Books Ltd.

Comte, A. (1975). Plan of the scientific operations necessary for reorganizing society. The Essential Writing, ed. Gertrud Lenzer. New York Harper Torch books, 57.

Davisson, E. M. (1997). Job satisfaction of secondary teachers as reported by self and principals. La Verne, California: University of La Verne Press.

DeSimone, R. (1998). Human resource development. 2nd ed. Orlando, FL: Dryden Press.

Dickens, N. L. (1998). A theory of action perspective of action research. Austin, Texas: University of Austin, 44-62.

Elworthy, J. S. (1999). The social origins of uncertainty: Popular struggles over science and truth in america, 1870-1914. New Brunswick, New Jersey: Grraduate School of New Brunswick Rutgers.

Fujii, M. (1999). The constructs of quality of life for cancer patients: Exploring factors that affect quality of life. St. Louis, Missouri: Washington University Press.

Gomberg, W. (1957). The use of psychology in industry: A trade union point of view, Management Science, 348-370.

Gray, J. L. & Starke, F. A. (1988). Organizational behavior (4th ed.). New York: Merrill.

Hackey, M. K. (1991). Injuries and illness in the workplace, 1989. Monthly Labor Review, 114(5), 34-36.

Hall, T. D. (1976). A system pathology of an organization: The rise and fall of the old saturday evening post. Administrative Science Quarterly, 21, 185-211.

Hall, T. D. (1979). A model of coping with role conflict: The role behavior of college educated women. Administrative Science Quarterly, 471-485.

Hall, T. D. (1986). Career development in organizations. San Francisco: Jossey-Bass.

Hall, T. D. (1987). Change in schools: facilitating the process. New York, New York: SUNY Press.

Hall, T. D. (1989). Social change in the southwest. Kansas: University Press of Kansas.

Hall, T. D. (1996). What's new in career management. Organizational Dynamics, 17-33.

Hall, T. D. (1997a). Change within an organization. Journal of Organizational Design, 237-268.

Hall, T. D. (1997b). Management and organizational behavior. 4th ed. New York: John Wiley & Sons, 385.

Hall, T. D., Bowen, D. D., Hall, Lewicki, J. R. and Hall, S. F. (1997). Experiences in management and organizational behavior. New York: John Wiley and Sons.

Harrington, B. J. (2000). Organizational learning: A theoretical overview and case study. Boston, Mass: Boston University, 34.

Hayden, V. M. (1998). Organizational revitalization and the management of change. Phoenix Arizona: Arizona State University, 2, 29, 34,57.

Hendry, C. (1996). Understanding and creating whole organizational change through learning theory. Human Relations, 621-641.

Herzberg, F. (1959). The motivation to work (2nd ed.). New York: John Wiley & Sons, 7, 111.

Herzberg, F. (1966). Work and the nature of man. Cleveland, OH: World Publishing Company.

Herzberg, F. (1976). The managerial choice: To be efficient and to be human. Homewood, IL: Dow Jones-Irwin.

Herzberg, F. (1982). The managerial choice: To be efficient and to be human. Homewood, IL: Dow-Jones-Irwin.

Herzberg, F. (1987). One more time: How do you motivate employees. Harvard Business Review (Sep.-Oct.): 109-120.

Herzberg, F., Monsner, B., & Snyderman, B. (1959). The motivation to work. New York: Wiley, 58-113.

Hesselbein, F., Goldsmith, M. and Beckhard, R. (1996). Leader of the future. San Francisco: Jossey-Bass Publishers.

Holsinger, B. D. (1973). The elementary school as modernizer: a Brazilian study. International Journal of Comparative Sociology, 180-202.

Hopp, A. Ellis, G., & Crossley, J. (1988). Employment motive of summer job seekers in recreation settings: A test of Herzberg's motivation-hygiene theory. Journal of Park and Recreation Administration, 6, 66-77.

Houghton, M. (1985). American heritage dictionary. Boston, MASS: Houghton Mifflin Company. Pp.476, 1218, 1335.

Inkeles, A. and Smith, H. D. (1974). Becoming modern. Cambridge: Harvard University Press.

Jenkins, J. A. (1990). Self-directed work force promotes safety. HR Magazine, 35(2), 54-56.

Jones, H. D. (1997). The panorama from point sublime: John wesley powell's religion of science and the intellectual origins of his arid lands reforms. Indiana University: Graduate School of Indiana University.

Kahl, A. J. (1968). The measurement of modernism. Austin: University of Texas Press, 4.

Khaldun, I. (1967). The muqaddimah: an introduction to history. Franz Rosenthal, ed. N.J. Dawood. Princeton: Princeton University Press, 45.

Kimmerling, G. F. (1985). Warning: Workers at risk, train effectively. Training and Development Journal, 39(4), 50-55.

Kolakowski, L. (1968). The alienation of reason: A history of positivist thought. Trans. Norbert Guterman Garden City, New York: Douleday & Compnay, Inc.

Kotter, P. J. (1996). Leading change. Boston. Mass: Harvard Business School Press.

Krikorian, H. D. (1997). Individual and group normative forces in small group decision-making processes: A time series analysis of a dynamic communication model. Santa Barbara, Cal.: University of Cal. Santa Barbara.

Kubler-Ross, E. & Kessler, D. (2000). Life lessons. New York: Scribner.

Kubler-Ross, E. (1969). On death and dying. New York: Collier Books, 41-43, 64-98, 342-343.

Kubler-Ross, E. (1983). On Children and death. New York: MacMillan Publishing Company, 61.

Kubler-Ross, E. (1997). On death and dying. New York: Scribner.

Lacey, P. K. (2000). Applicability of Herzberg's motivation hygiene theory to public high school principles in the state of Maryland. Maryland: George Washington University.

Lauer, H. R. (1990). Perspectives on social change. Columbus, OH: Allen and Bacon.

Lawler, E. E. (1973). Motivation in work organizations. Monterey, CA.: Brooks/Cole. 25.

Leath, B. D. (2000). Workplace involvement: Common forces, attributes, and outcomes within a maximum heterogeneous sample of highly involved employees. Union Institute Press, 260-261.

Lewin, K. (1935). A dynamic theory of personality. New York: McGraw-Hill Book Company, 80-83.

Lewin, K. (1936). Principles of topological psychology. New York:

McGraw-Hall, 5-41.

Lewin, K. (1944). The dynamics of group action. Educational Leadership, 195-200.

Lewin, K. (1947). Frontiers in-group dynamics. Human Relations, 5-41, 87-95, 237-242.

Lewin, K. (1951). Field theory in social science. New York: Harper & Row, 228-229.

Lewin, K. (1952) Group decision and social change. In G.E. Swanson, T.E. Newcomb, & E.L. Hartlet (eds.), Readings in social psychology. New York: Holt Rinehart, 459-473.

Lewin, K. (1958). Field theory in social sciences. New York: Harper and Row, 115.

Lewin, K., Dembo, T. and Barker, R. (1976). Frustration and regression: An experiment with young children. Iowa City, Iowa: University of Iowa Press, 6.

Lippitt, R., Watson, J., & Westley, B. (1958). The dynamics of planned change. New York: Harcourt, Brace & World, 100.

Lurie, K. S. (2000). Employee learning in dynamic work settings: An exploration of adult learning in business organizations. Fielding Institute, 32.

Luthans, F. (1985). Organizational behavior. New York: McGraw-Hill.

Magnuson, C. (1992). Motives for working in a non-traditional organizational summer camp job: A test of the content theories. University of Minnesota: Minnesota.

Marrow, A. (1969). The practical theorist. New York: Basic Books, Inc.

Maslow, A. (1942). The dynamics of psychological security-insecurity. Character and Personality, 10(4), 331-344.

Maslow, A. (1943). A theory of human motivation. Psychological review, 50, 370-396.

Maslow, A. (1954). Motivation and personality. New York: Harper and Row, 90.

Maslow, A. (1957). Two kinds of cognition and their integration. General semantics Bulletin, 20/21, 17-22.

Maslow, A. (1958). Emotional blocks to creativity. Journal of Individual Psychology, 14, 51-56.

Maslow, A. (1959). New knowledge in human values. New York:

Harper.

Maslow, A. (1962). Lessons from the peal-experiences. Journal of Humanistic Psychology, 2(1), 9-18.

Maslow, A. (1967). Self-actualization and beyond. In J.F.T. Bugental (Ed.), Challenges of humanistic psychology. New York: McGraw-Hill, 279-286.

Maslow, A. (1968). Toward a psychology of being. New York: Van Nostrand Reinhold.

Maslow, A. (1968a). Toward a psychology of being (2nd ed.). New York: Van Nostrand Reinhold.

Maslow, A. (1970). Motivation and personality. New York: Harper & Bros., 2nd edition.

Maslow, A. (1973). The farther reaches of human nature. London: Penguin.

Maslow, A.(1980). Donkeys and sticks. Nephrology Nurse, 21.

Mayes, B. T. (1978, January). Some boundary considerations in the application of motivation models. Academy of Management Review, pp. 51-52.

McCarthy, C. F. (1997). A study of the factors which affect job satisfaction and job dissatisfaction in public school teachers. Seattle, WA: Seattle Pacific University.

McClellan, C. (1999). Science, intellect, and social evolution: A study of auguste comte's philosophy of science. Note Dame, Indiana: University of Norte Dame.

Miller, N. (1951). Learnable drives and rewards. Handbook of Experimental Psychology. New York: Wiley.

Mills, V. J. (1999). Resistance to corporate change: Perceptions of first-level supervisors and customer service employees. New York, New York: New York University.

Morgan, G. (1997). Images of organization. Thousand Oaks, California: Sage Publications, 294.

Morgan, H. O. (2000). A study of job satisfaction and work related variables of special education teachers in Idaho. University of Idaho Press, 32.

Neufeldt, V. and Guralnik, B. D. (1988). Webster's new world dictionary. 3rd College Edition. New York, New York: Simon & Schuster, Inc.

Oleson, M. (1999). Using maslow's needs model to assess individuals attitudes towards money. Logan, Utah: Utah State University.

Piaget, J. & Rolanda, G. (1989). Psychogenesis and the history of science. Trans. Helga Feider. New York: Columbia University Press.

Rafferty, C. E. (1999). Apostle of human progress: The life of lester frank ward. Providence, Rhode Island: Washington University of St. Louis.

Roberts, S. C. (1997). Leading change to create the future: A comparative case study of nasa and xerox. Los Angeles, California: University of Southern California, 234.

Rothwell, W. J. (1989). Complying with OSHA. Training and Development Journal, 43(5), 52-54.

Schneider, B. & Bowen, D. E. (1995). Winning the service game. Boston: Harvard Business School Press.

Schneider, S., Benjamin, J., Alderfer, C. P., Clayton, P. (1973). Three studies of measures of need satisfaction in organizations. Administrative Science Quarterly. New York: Ithaca.

Schwartz, H. S. (1983). A theory of deontic work motivation. Journal of Applied Behavioral Science, 19(2), 203-214.

Schweiger, D., Ivancevich, J. and Power, F. (1987). Executive actions for managing human resource before and after acquisition. Academy of Management Executive, 1, 2, 127-138.

Seguin, M. (1997). Motivation, job satisfaction, needs, and vocational preferences urban secondary teachers and administrators. Windsor, Canada: Windsor University Press, 117.

Simpson, G. (1969). Sire of sociology. New York: Thomas Y. Crowell Company.

Smith, C., & Comer. D. (1994). Self-organizing in small groups: A study of group effectiveness with non-equilibrium conditions. Human Relations, 47, 553-581.

Soleiman-Panah, M. S. (1999). The foucault shift in sociological theory: From epistemological to ontological critique. British Columbia, Canada: University of British Columbia.

Somervell, A. (1961). A study of history. Volumes 6-10, 338.

Sorokin, A. P. (1941). The crisis of our age. New York: Dutton, 173-252

Sorokin, A. P. (1947). Social and cultural dynamics. New York: American Book Company, 87.

Spencer, H. (1851). Social statics. London: Chapman, 19-23.

Spencer, H. (1874). The study of sociology. New York: D. Appleton & Company, 401- 404.

Spencer, H. (1880). The study of sociology. New York: D. Appleton, 366-367.

Spencer, H. (1883). Notice of dynamic sociology. Glimpses of the Cosmos, Vol III, 213

Spencer, H. (1892). The principles of ethics, I. 2 vols. London: Williams and Northgate, 26.

Spencer, H. (1938). First principles, part II, chapter I, The story of social philosophy. New York: Prentice Hall, 442.

Spencer, H. (1955). The principles of psychology, 2nd edn, 2 vols. London: Longmans, 500-502.

Spencer, H. (1965). Society and personality. England Cliffs, NJ.: Prentice-Hall, 393.

Spencer, H. (1969). Principles of sociology. London: MacMillan, 29.

Spencer, H. (1988). Evolutionary theory. American Journal of Sociology 93, 154.

Spencer. H. (1894). Principles of biology, 2nd edn, 2 vols. Londoen: Williams and Northgate.

Toynbee, A. (1946). A study of history. NY: Oxford University Press.

Toynbee, A. (1957). Study of history. New York: Oxford University, 283.

Toynbee, A. (1961). Reconsiderations. New York: Oxford University Press, 198.

Vitucci, S. S. (1996). Patterns of influence: A study of the founding fathers of organizational development. Austin, Texas: University of Austin, 56.

Webster's New World Dictionary of America (1988). New York: Simon & Schuster, 889.

Weick, K. E. (1969). The social psychology of organizing. Reading, Mass.: Addison-Wesley.

Weisbord, M. (1989). Productive workplaces. San Francisco, CA: Jossey Bass.

Wesley, T. M. (1996). Teachers' concerns and voluntary adoption activities in educational technology innovation. Mississippi: Mississippi State University.

White, D. D. and Bednar, A. D. (1986). Organizational Behavior: Understanding and managing people at work. Newton, MASS: Allyn and Bacon.

Wilson, S. L. (1996). A summative evaluation of the implementation of total quality management in a military medical organization. Walden University, 29-35.

Zimmerman, B. & Armstrong, R. (1994). Remembering the future: Creating change-ability at Linda Lundstrom Ltd. North York, ON: York University Faculty of Administrative Studies.

The Author

Dr. Robert DuPrey has written many books including university textbooks; He has also written business articles covering technologies and business management organization. He has earned his doctorate degree in Business Organization and a Masters Degree in Business Administration. He currently resides in Southern California and is acting as Sr. business consultant and advisor to the Government of the United States of America and many private American and European organizations.

BASIS FOR
MOTIVATION
AND
CHANGE

This Book

This book presents a comprehensive view of the change and the change models and provides detail analysis of the social, business and individual change aspects and theories.

-Motivation Theories
-Change Models
-Organizational Change
-Social Change
-Individual Change